King's Gallery

Living **Words** *1*

Presented To:

_____

With Love:

_____

On:

_____

Dedicated to all those who long for the real experience of True Love... And the God who delivers.

King's Gallery

Living Words 1

Troi Cockayne

King's Gallery

Living Words 1

ISBN-13: 978-0692517536
ISBN-10: 0692517537

Published by King's Gallery. Available from Amazon.com, CreateSpace.com and other online stores.

Reviews

"These revelations from Troi Cockayne are all fresh as a walk with God. They are inspirations from a man who knows the fellowship of divine love."
~ Imogen Mordecai, Cambridge, United Kingdom.

"After 45 years in ministry, it has been hard to find many Christian writers and speakers who had the latest word from the Father's heart. You my brother are one of those rare gifted servants of God that speaks directly to my heart, spirit, and soul. I grow closer and closer to my Father because of your obedience in communicating what Abba is speaking to His last day warriors. I want the book, Gracias. We need the truth He speaks through you." *~ Joseph Almaraz, Las Vegas, Nevada. USA.*

"As a former Muslim I was fully immersed into the world of religion. When I became a Christian I understood freedom, but wasn't exempt from the trials of life. In some of my most hopeless moments, where I could fully relate to the words of King David "why are you so cast down O my soul," Troi's Love Journal Entries were a breath of fresh air that carried freedom from all religious bondages; from past or present. Each entry was a secret glimpse into the heart of God and gave me hope to carry on, to move forward and just let God saturate and overtake me." *~ Mo Ka. Vancouver, BC, Canada.*

"Troi your inspiring words have been straight from heaven pouring encouragement and hope upon me and others as we press through life's journey. You are truly a vessel that living waters flow out of. Through your own trials, anointed to bring life, encouragement, love and hope to all that have ears to hear, speaking straight to our hearts. Bless you bountifully my brother in Christ Jesus. Truly the love of Jesus flows through you."
~ Deborah Popoff Terlap. Gurnee, Illinois, USA.

"Troi's words always brings comfort and a feeling that my GOD is speaking just to me through him. Thank you, Troi for writing and sharing these precious words. Can't wait to get a copy of your book!" *~ Cherie Martin-Grimes. Gig Harbor, Washington, USA.*

"These inspired words, are words flowing directly from the Father's heart to His children. Words that inspired me personally, to look deep within, to the truth that has already been planted there. Words that inspire to keep seeking the truth of God's love within you, that's been poured out by His Spirit. Freedom always follows when God's love and truth is embraced." ~ *Anushka Amanda. Eloff Hennings, South Africa.*

"Your journal posts have been used greatly in my life. Your passion for the world to personally experience the deep and wide love of the Father has been contagious! I have been filled to overflowing by the rawness of your expression. You are a genuine vessel, a glorious conduit of the grace of our Majestic God. My walk has been strengthened by your authenticity and I have been thoroughly encouraged. Glory to the King!" ~ *Christina Rosser. Kirkland, Washington, USA.*

"I have been following you for over 9 months and there wasn't a post of your's that didn't speak to me some how, some way. God has truly used you in a mighty way. Straight to the heart each time. I always ask myself wow, how did he know I needed to hear that?! Ha ha…You're encouraging. I anticipate your entries daily. May Our LORD keep you and your family encouraging others daily God knows we need it." ~ *Sheila, Vacaville, CA, USA.*

"Very refreshing, very different from the normal theological language and approach. More intimate, personal and realistic. A desperate person, craving and longing for that 'one real love'." ~ *Annie Sandhya, India.*

"I search for your journal entries on Facebook because they enrich the quality of my life. They speak words that my heart had been feeling but couldn't clarify. Your revelations are "Rama' words for me and ignite my spirit and soul. Thank you for feeding me manna that I look forward to eating each day. Journey is my word because you are an answered prayer of mine." ~ *Monah L Callahan, Kentucky, USA.*

You have an intimate relationship with our Lord Jesus Christ. Your love for Him is clearly evident and it is expressed not only through your posts, but as well as through the magnificent sculptures you so wonderfully create as to tell a story, inspire, encourage and deeply touch the hearts of believers and non-believers alike. Even in the times of the storm, you always manage to stay focused and have your eyes firmly set upon "the Rock on whom we all stand." ~ *Suzana Hrisik Seremetkovska, Sydney, Australia.*

King's Gallery

Living Words *1*

"These things I have spoken to you while abiding with you. But the Helper, the Holy Spirit, whom the Father will send in My name, He will teach you all things, and bring to your remembrance all that I said to you."
John 14:25-26 NASB

"My sheep hear My voice, and I know them, and they follow Me; and I give eternal life to them, and they will never perish."
John 10:27-28 NASB

Then he said, 'The God of our fathers has appointed you to know His will, to see the Righteous One, and to hear the sound of His voice.'
Acts 22:14 HCSB

King's Gallery

Introduction

"Take My yoke upon you and learn from Me,
for I am gentle and humble in heart, and you will find rest for your souls."
Matthew 11:29 NASB

This is a personal invitation of the living God, echoing to each of us *personally*, as if to say "Will you allow Me to walk with you, right by your side and speak to your heart the things that matter most?" God has sent His Son not to put the weight of condemnation and guilt, but God sent His Son to lift us all into the light of True Love.

For God did not send His Son into the world that He might condemn the world,
but that the world might be saved through Him.
John 3:17 HCSB

King's Gallery

King's Gallery, Living Words *1* is the first book in a collection of books displaying journal entries of Troi Cockayne. Each entry came forth as a gentle whisper from God. Whispering hope, healing comfort and deep affection. In the following pages, heavenly revelation dovetails with confirming scriptures and beautiful imagery like love songs. This book is simply a beautiful symphony of those *living words* resounding to the personal heart. As they wash over you, may the deepening awareness of God's presence ignite real faith, hope and love in your life.

The Word became flesh and made his dwelling among us. We have seen his glory, the glory of the one and only Son, who came from the Father, full of grace and truth.
John 1:14

King's Gallery

Greatest Discovery

For twenty years I 'learned' about the word of God at church. But in my deepest, darkest broken heart I met the *Living Word* of God on the pages of my tear stained journals. My *greatest discovery* in my greatest hour of need, in the deepest pit of my life when no one was there, not even a pastor—Jesus was there. I had never owned a journal prior to 2010 and had no desire to write. In the midst of that darkest time of my life, a friend recommended I purchase a journal and write in it. This did not appeal to me at all. But in respect for the man and my desperate need for anything that would help me in my pain I agreed to buy a journal and cry out on its pages. What I discovered through the many hours of writing my thoughts, prayers and petitions, along with writing scriptures that spoke to my heart and revelations that also came to mind was that the *Living Word* and the tangible presence of love met me in my greatest hour of need. I do not consider myself a writer as much as I am a *desperate listener* for *True Love*. I have nothing to boast. It is the grace of God that in the midst of my own brokenness that I would discover and hear such beautiful words of wisdom and comfort. When He speaks, His words are full of life, love and encouragement.

King's Gallery

I began to realize that God was so much more than my Sunday 'boxed' version of Him and that Jesus truly was with me. Not just in a wide corporate sense, but with me in the most *personal* sense. To find the personal presence of God being truly *with me* and not just an impersonal religious truth, has forever changed my life. I pray that my testimony will encourage many to fully understand that the true purpose of the life, death and resurrection of Christ was not so much that we would go to church each week, as much as it was to restore each one of us back into *intimacy* with God. True Love is here now and He wants us to know Him *personally*. Each of the words in this collection were spoken to me within the context of real fears, real tears, trials and tribulations. The continual encouraging power of these words, even years after the passing circumstances is truly amazing to me. For this reason I share them with you. My hope is to encourage as many people as possible and lead them to the *intimate heart* of God, found in Christ Jesus. May their seemingly timeless comfort touch yours and your families hearts for years to come. My sincerest prayer is that you would buy a journal yourself and let the *Living Word* meet with you on its pages.

~ Troi Cockayne

King's Gallery

Books Purpose

What I heard the Holy Spirit say to me about the purpose of sharing these journal entries in book form—

"It is My hearts desire that each of My children would come to know My intimate care and love in their deepest hearts. The inner most thoughts and feelings is the place I long to enter with My *True Love*. Lonely and broken is a life lived without True Love restored. I am not like man with shifting shadows. My love is true and heals a life-time of pain caused by mans dysfunction. All is vanity and chasing the wind apart from the truth of these very words. My love brings vibrant life to the broken heart and its greatest blessing is found in intimacy with My words and My presence. Church is good, but is no substitute for daily soaking intimacy. I fill your cup for the day at hand like manna in the wilderness. Daily dependence is by design."

~ Love journal entry, Troi Cockayne.

King's Gallery

Unique Song

There's a place that God Himself wants to walk with and talk with only you. There is a *unique song* that your life with God was meant to sing. Unique creative beauty like artwork with God. Our life the brush—His hand that moves us. Beauty from ashes is the masterpiece that God alone creates in the human heart that turns to Him. Thank you Jesus for my pen, my hand in yours. You alone are the Living Word and you meet the open heart that hears its flow.

A love song. My heart is moved by a noble theme as I recite my verses to the king;
my tongue is the pen of a skillful writer.
Psalm 45:1 HCSB

For those who are led by the Spirit of God are the children of God.
Romans 8:14

For no prophecy was ever produced by the will of man,
but men spoke from God as they were carried along by the Holy Spirit.
2 Peter 1:21 ESV

King's Gallery

Words

Of all the *words* spoken to you, are there any more important than My words to you? Sift words and see the ones that belong to Me. Know My voice above all others. I hold the path of life and I AM the giver of all good and perfect gifts. No one has ever loved you like I love you. I created you to be in relationship with Me. Hear My words of love to you, for they will fill you and lead you to life eternal. Are there any words more important?

In the beginning was the Word, and the Word was with God, and the Word was God.
John 1:1

The Word became flesh and made his dwelling among us.
John 1:14

For the word of God is quick, and powerful, and sharper than any twoedged sword, piercing even to the dividing asunder of soul and spirit, and of the joints and marrow, and is a discerner of the thoughts and intents of the heart.
Hebrews 4:12 KJV

"The grass withers, the flowers fade, but the word of our God remains forever."
Isaiah 40:8 HCSB

King's Gallery

Pen and Paper

Pen and paper is critical for clarity. I give you pieces of your destiny on its pages. My hand in yours will bring you comfort and confidence. This is an exercise in open intimacy with My voice to *you* personally. I hold the plans for your life and I long to give its detail. Posture yourself at My feet and I will indeed speak to your heart. My love and My voice brings confirmation and dissipates the dark clouds of confusion, fear and depression. Rise up in this My child and I will carry you into its reality. Your journal is the table-top for the puzzle pieces of your life.

"For I know the plans I have for you," declares the Lord,
"Plans to prosper you and not to harm you, plans to give you hope and a future."
Jeremiah 29:11

Now we see things imperfectly, like puzzling reflections in a mirror, but then we will see everything with perfect clarity. All that I know now is partial and incomplete, but then I will know everything completely, just as God now knows me completely.
1 Corinthians 13:12 NLT

And the LORD answered me:
"Write the vision; make it plain on tablets, so he may run who reads it."
Habakkuk 2:2 ESV

King's Gallery

Not Alone

I have not left you. Do not be dismayed at this season I have placed you in. I put the pieces of your divine design together. Everything comes together in its due time. See My faithfulness in creation and know My children have My greatest affection. The buds of a new season have already begun to form in your life. Be patient, it won't be long and the world will see My miracle life manifested out of the destruction of your former life. Trust My timing. I know the seasons of your life. I have you and your children. I cover your life. Release the fear that you are not covered and cared for. I AM with you in every moment of your day. Awaken to this reality. Accept the truth of My ever present love for you and over you. You are *not alone.*

He will cover you with his feathers, and under his wings you will find refuge;
his faithfulness will be your shield and rampart.
Psalm 91:4

"Be strong and courageous. Do not fear or be in dread of them, for it is the LORD
your God who goes with you. He will not leave you or forsake you."
Deuteronomy 31:6 ESV

Isaiah 41:10, John 14:16-18

King's Gallery

Ark of Presence

Soak in My instruction each day, then move out. Let the water of My words carry your boat into your day, it beats rowing on the sand of self. The ark of My presence is the structure that carries the life. All activity outside the 'ark' of My presence leads to death. Abide in My love and My wisdom. Divine design and destiny are accomplished when you are in alignment with My will and My word.

But seek ye first the kingdom of God, and his righteousness;
and all these things shall be added unto you.
Matthew 6:33 KJV

As the Father has loved me, so have I loved you. Abide in my love.
John 15:9 ESV

Listen to my instruction and be wise; do not disregard it.
Proverbs 8:33

By faith Noah, when warned about things not yet seen,
in holy fear built an ark to save his family.
Hebrews 11:7

9

King's Gallery

Children of Light

You are *children of light*. To walk this path, stay in agreement with heaven and do not turn to the right or to the left. Walk by faith, not by sight. Do not trust what you see or be rocked by circumstance. Children of light walk through darkness and the wreckage of sin and death. Speak to these bones to live! Call healing where there is sickness, call light where there is darkness and speak life where there is death. Heaven is your reality. Do not look at the things that are seen, but the things that are unseen. Speak My will. Faith is heavens currency and I have given you a full measure. With Me you have more than enough. Take back what the enemy has stolen. You are My arms, My legs, My mouth. Speak, walk, touch! You have the mind of Christ. You have walked in the natural. I am calling you to walk in the Supernatural! The kingdom of darkness can not stand against My body when it is awake. And so I say to you awake, awake! Arise! My blood flows to My body to bring life. Believe Me when I say, you speak life or death. Speak life. Ask according to My will and it shall be done. The armies of heaven await your words!

Ephesians 5:8-11, John 14:13, Ezekiel 37:4, Philippians 2:15, John 8:12

King's Gallery

My Lions

A mind fixed on Me, moves with power and great courage. The fear of man has no power on *My Lions*. The righteous are as bold as lions. You were not created for fear and foolishness, but for bold, righteous Love. I have made you strong. I have made you faithful. I have made you fearless. I have made you disciplined. I have made you in My image; perfect love. Now rise up and fall into agreement and alignment with My word, for Truth has spoken. Do not shrink back from this with an unbelieving heart. I clothe you in My righteousness. I wash shame and guilt away in My sacrificial love for you. *Awake* My child and shake off the lies that separate you from My love. I AM the lion of the tribe of Judah. Rise up in My power and love. Never back down and never give up!

"Be strong and courageous. Do not be afraid or terrified because of them,
for the LORD your God goes with you; he will never leave you nor forsake you."
Deuteronomy 31:6

"But as for you, be strong and do not give up, for your work will be rewarded."
2 Chronicles 15:7

The wicked flee though no one pursues, but the righteous are as bold as a lion.
Proverbs 28:1

13

King's Gallery

Tie Your Heart

Give Me your undivided attention that your heart may take in My complete acceptance of you. Engage yourself to My deep affection for you. Marry your heart to My perfect love for you and put on My sound mind, that we may become one together. Solid connection is the bedrock of My kingdom. True love is undiluted by the empty distractions of the world. Whole hearts connected in My real, deep love establishes My kingdom of true lovers. Sincere and saturated, they carry the river of My Spirit. *Tie your heart* to Mine, unadulterated by the world. Those devoted to True Love receive the benefits of *true love* and the atmosphere of heaven.

For your Maker is your husband—the LORD Almighty is his name—
the Holy One of Israel is your Redeemer; he is called the God of all the earth.
Isaiah 54:5

Let us be glad and rejoice, and give honor to him: for the marriage of the Lamb
is come, and his wife hath made herself ready. And to her was granted that she should
be arrayed in fine linen, clean and white: for the fine linen is the righteousness of saints.
Revelation 19:7-9 KJV

Isaiah 54:5, Revelations 21:9, Luke 5:16, Luke 10:38-42

King's Gallery

Cocoon

How big is your God child? *Cocoon* in the light of My presence. Allow Me to saturate your mind with heavens reality. I will show you a better way. Complete submission to the cocoon of divine design is the only pathway to its reality. Relinquish all of your crawling ways. Attach to Me, The Vine, and cocoon in My love. I will transform your heart. Allow Me to download your divine purpose. Quietly submit and attach to My love. Listen to the inspiration of My Spirit, My voice...

"Behold, I AM the LORD, the God of all flesh. Is anything too hard for Me?"
Jeremiah 32:27 ESV

Do not conform to the pattern of this world, but be transformed by the renewing of your mind. Then you will be able to test and approve what God's will is—
his good, pleasing and perfect will.
Romans 12:2

He will transform the body of our humble condition into the likeness of His glorious body, by the power that enables Him to subject everything to Himself.
Philippians 3:21 HCSB

" I AM the Vine; you are the branches. If you remain in me and I in you, you will bear much fruit; apart from me you can do nothing."
John 15:5

17

King's Gallery

Lap of Love

Lets ride this ride together. You can sit on My lap. Your life will go through many hills and valleys. Know My love sits with you. Do not shrink back with fear, but grab the bar of your life with excitement! Where we are going will exhilarate you. Know you are safe in My arms. Even death is just a door to My eternal life. I've got you My child. Do not ever forget this truth. Sit with Me and I will sit with you. Your awareness of My presence is your greatest possession. Rest in My Love above all else. Be obedient to My instructions, even in the midst of fear. Know My voice. Find time to sit and sift My words.

*And God raised us up with Christ and seated us with him
in the heavenly realms in Christ Jesus.*
Ephesians 2:6

*"On that day you will realize that I am in my Father,
and you are in me, and I am in you."*
John 14:20

Cast all your anxiety on him because he cares for you.
1 Peter 5:7

In you, LORD my God, I put my trust.
Psalm 25:1

King's Gallery

My Pens

I want to write *'Love'* all over the world. You are *My pens*. You were designed to be filled and to flow freely wherever I use you. A pen that works and then doesn't work is frustrating in the hand of it's master. So it is, with cursing and blessing, death and life, pride and love. This is faulty and a result of the fall of man. My original design for man was for constant flow of giving and receiving love. I came to restore that which has been blocked and broken, that once again My life would fill you and flow out from you onto a world that has lost it's *identity*. Write *'I am Love'* on your heart, then do the same to those around you. Do not forget your identity. The ink of My spirit flows reliable through those that receive and give it's reality. Write *'My Love'* on everything. Complete the sentence as it was intended. My words never falter and always produce truth which brings clarity. Confusion comes from fear and fear stems from lies. Guard your heart above all else for it is the wellspring of life. Submit to My filling and then flow onto others just as I have flowed onto you. Love as I have loved you. Speak and write *'Reliable Love'* with your life. My love is constant and eternal. My words always write Faithful and True. I seek to replicate My words and My life in you, My vessels of love.

King's Gallery

Intimate Abiding

Fret not thyself. Stand fast in My love and all My powers to save. Rejoice in this hour for what I am about to do, and do not give place to fear. Release your needs through prayer and I The Lord will indeed deliver you. Meditate on My promises and see My miracles all around you. *Release fear... Release anxiety...* They come to rob you of the purity of My peace. The minutes of your day are maximized in the atmosphere of My love. Fruit is born from your *intimate abiding,* that will feed those with whom you have contact. Nothing is more important than your solid connection to My sound mind. Let there be no gaps or disconnects to our solid engagement. Realize the troubles of this world will pass away, but My love for you will never pass away. Abide in My love despite the storms and see My powers to calm the elements of trouble.

"I have told you these things, so that in me you may have peace.
In this world you will have trouble. But take heart! I have overcome the world."
John 16:33

"And call on me in the day of trouble; I will deliver you, and you will honor me."
Psalm 50:15

Yet I will exult in the LORD, I will rejoice in the God of my salvation.
Habakkuk 3:18 NASB

King's Gallery

Eternal Value

For those who value eternal peace, you will sit with Eternal Peace. For those who value eternal love, you will abide in My perfect love. For those who value the truth, you will search for it with all your heart. For those who value the way to life, you will value the words of a *resurrected man*. People will always gravitate and spend time around what they value. The wise will value what should be valued. My words have value because they are life and lead to life eternal. Those who seek Me find life. Press into My love and you too, will experience the life to come. Those who do not come to Me remain in death, and it is for this reason I say come. My love and life is for all who would receive Me. There is indeed only one way for sinful man to come into holy, righteous, perfect love and that is through My sacrifice. 'For there is one God and one mediator between God and man—The man Christ Jesus.' This is My true word and I do not lie. Those who reject My word reject truth and the only way to eternal life. Mercy is a gift given by My real sacrifice. To spend a life and not consider 'The way, the truth, and the life' is to remain in death. I AM the light of life. Those who come to Me will not walk in darkness or the shadow of death.

John 6:63, 1 Timothy 2:5, Deuteronomy 30:15, Proverbs 10:2

King's Gallery

Crossing the Jordon

Sitting with Me is your single most important work. I will disclose the secrets of My kingdom and your divine purpose. It is My desire to give you the keys to My kingdom. Have great confidence in My ability to bring the pieces. Submit your days to Me like steps. I will give you solid footing on My word. Step forward into the Jordan My child, it is time.

*'Call to Me and I will answer you and tell you great
and unsearchable things you do not know.'
Jeremiah 33:3*

*"I will give you the keys of the kingdom of heaven,
and whatever you bind on earth is already bound in heaven,
and whatever you loose on earth is already loosed in heaven."
Matthew 16:19 HCSB*

*And the priests who carried the ark of the covenant of the LORD stood firm
on dry ground in the middle of the Jordan while all Israel crossed on dry ground,
until all the nation had finished crossing the Jordan.
Joshua 3:17 NASB*

King's Gallery

My Lights

Your lives are lights... A flashing picture of My eternal love, taken in the mind of My life-giving Spirit. Shine My stars of hope to the hurting world around you. Ha-ha! Laughter, dancing in the hearts of My children, taking hold of Joy! Sing, laugh, and dance in freedom, My songs of love! Resound in the valleys... Resound in the mountains... Resound in the hearts of the hurting... Sing it aloud, with no reservations, My love unstoppable! I AM with all of you My children. Who can stop what we do together? Love is our weapon, and all the forces of hell can not stop love—'The light of the world'. In the face of dark hate, shine love. You hold the greatest power in the universe, My love.

You are the light of the world. A city built on a hill cannot be hidden.
Neither do people light a lamp and put it under a bowl. Instead they put it on its stand,
and it gives light to everyone in the house. In the same way, let your light shine before
others, that they may see your good deeds and glorify your Father in heaven.
Matthew 5:14-16

When Jesus spoke again to the people, he said, "I am the light of the world.
Whoever follows me will never walk in darkness, but will have the light of life."
John 8:12

King's Gallery

Grace Soil

This is a special time set apart that you may learn to hear My voice. Wrestle through this, for it is My purpose to guide your mind into life itself. Know My heart. Know My tone of love. Hear the pace and the peace in My voice. Do not be discouraged when things go wrong. I have you in My hands. Grace is the soil of growth I plant you in. I do not condemn your mistakes. Simply look to Me, your teacher. I see you through the eyes of love. Be released from the voices of criticism and condemnation, the voices of your past, the voices that seek to rob your soul. The enemy seeks to accuse and stop you from coming to Me. Allow the truth of My love to wash you of your past failures. Failure is a part of learning and I do not condemn. I encourage your steps. Go easy on yourself in this process. Grace for yourself and for others is the rich soil of My kingdom, where many flowers bloom. Take root in Me and allow the nutrients of My love to saturate your thoughts. The enemy has used the disobedient to speak words of death and discouragement throughout your life. These are weeds that must be removed and uprooted from your heart and mind. Mine is the voice of perfect love and there is no shadow of turning with Me. My love for you is constant and unwavering, it never changes. Listen to Me and find rest for your soul. I came to set you free from sin and death and give you... My very life.

King's Gallery

Bloom

Like rivers in the desert, I spring forth new life to your parched land. Drink of My Spirit, and life will indeed come forth. Saturate your soil in My love for you. Open to Me, that My son-light may kiss your heart. Release the weight of the world and come to Me. I will give you rest. The season of My deliverance is at hand. Take heed to My instruction, for My words are life and will lead *the way*. I Alone raise up and tear down. Nothing is hidden from My eyes. I will heal your land. *Bloom* in the glory of My presence and open wide your heart. Love calls forth the fruit of your life.

I will make rivers flow on barren heights, and springs within the valleys.
I will turn the desert into pools of water, and the parched ground into springs.
Isaiah 41:18

It will burst into bloom; it will rejoice greatly and shout for joy.
The glory of Lebanon will be given to it, the splendor of Carmel and Sharon;
they will see the glory of the LORD, the splendor of our God.
Isaiah 35:2

John 7:38, 2 Chronicles 7:14

King's Gallery

Eyes of Faith

Learning to settle into My peace and My presence is your greatest activity. See what I show you. I know the way to your destiny and abundant provision. Narrow is the way that leads to life and few find it. Consider a lifetime of activity and effort outside of My life; doctor, lawyer, president, wealth, pleasure. Your lives are but vapors that appear for a moment and then dissipate. Generations and generations have come and gone. Swirling activity and effort, 'chasing the wind'. All is meaningless apart from My wisdom and My life. I created man to be in constant communion with Me, his creator. I AM Perfect Love. Divine design and order are My ways. I Jesus AM the key that bridges the gap for mans dysfunction and brokenness. I share My heart and Life and show the way. What god is like your God? I permeate all things with My wisdom. *All* work and effort and life comes to nothing apart from My will. All efforts to reach Me and others through My love will have eternal impact. *Eyes of faith* child, eyes of faith. My eyes see eternal things and so will yours, more and more.

But seek first His kingdom and His righteousness, and all these things
will be given to you as well.
Matthew 6:33

Ecclesiastes 2:11, Luke 10:41-42, John 14:6

King's Gallery

Kingdom Clarity

You are at the door of your destiny. Time with Me brings its clarity. Sift the sand of your life. Find the gold pieces that make up its walkway. You are My arms and legs. You know My heart. Move to its beat in alignment with its purpose. *Kingdom clarity* seeks to establish My dominion on earth as it is in heaven. Allow its backdrop to surface. Prepare your visual boats, your vessels of salvation, when it is time, I will send water. Use this time to sharpen your life. I have called you to a life of integrity and wisdom. 'Come up here', see with My eyes. Do not follow the flow of the world. My ways are higher than mans ways, and I say to you again 'Come up here'. I see from the vantage point of eternal life. Allow My perfect love to fill your heart and mind and drive out all your fears. Know I never leave you.

Then they heard a loud voice from heaven saying to them, "Come up here."
And they went up to heaven in a cloud, while their enemies looked on.
Revelation 11:12

Noah did everything just as God commanded him.
The Lord then said to Noah, "Go into the ark, you and your whole family,
because I have found you righteous in this generation."
Genesis 6:22

King's Gallery

Beautiful Miracles

I see with deep love. One person has infinite value in My eyes. See deeply into the hearts of My children. See their beauty as I created them. Brush the sand of sin and death from them in love to see the treasure I created. Do for them what I have done for you. Stand in My Eternal Love and see them with My intended design. *Beautiful miracles,* untainted by the sickness of sin and death. I see amazing miracles. The light of My love awakens them to their beauty. The light of My love awakens belief, awakens hope...

This is the LORD'S doing; it is marvelous in our eyes.
Psalms 118:23 KJV

For you created my inmost being; you knit me together in my mother's womb.
I praise you because I am fearfully and wonderfully made;
your works are wonderful, I know that full well.
Psalm 139:13-14

For by one sacrifice he has made perfect forever those who are being made holy.
Hebrews 10:14

We love because He first loved us.
1 John 4:19 HCSB

39

King's Gallery

Grasping Thoughts

Many distractions have 'good' labels that captivate those who want to 'be good'. My love and My power is the only saving grace for mans dysfunction. The mire of sin and death surrounds My creation and I alone can raise you out. 'For there is one mediator between God and man, The man Christ Jesus.' But you must lay hold of My saving love with your *grasping thoughts*...What pulls you? Words are vehicles that lead your life to heaven or hell. Man is a trailer which follows the words that the mind attaches to. Secure your mind on My promises and My love for you will indeed lead to a 'future and a hope.'

"For I know the plans I have for you," declares the LORD,
"Plans to prosper you and not to harm you, plans to give you hope and a future."
Jeremiah 29:11

Set your minds on things that are above, not on things that are on earth.
Colossians 3:2 ESV

Finally brothers, whatever is true, whatever is honorable, whatever is just,
whatever is pure, whatever is lovely, whatever is commendable — if there is any moral
excellence and if there is any praise—dwell on these things. Do what you have learned
and received and heard and seen in me, and the God of peace will be with you.
Philippians 4:8 HCSB

King's Gallery

Love Display

Sacrifice and suffering that is motivated by sincere love displays My great power. Your offended self is dead and has no power. Your fearful self is dead and has no power. Your faithless self is dead and has no power. Your lustful self is dead and has no power. Calm fear with My love. Display My love by your actions. Your lazy self is dead. My diligent love is alive in you. My blood is prepared to act for My beloved. My heart is focused on what must be done to redeem My children. For the joy of the fruit of My death, I die. My heart sees My beloved. My actions display the level of My love for you. I came to display My wisdom, My power, and My love to My creation. I backed up My words with My actions. I have called you to arm yourself with the same mindset.

Greater love has no one than this: to lay down one's life for one's friends.
John 15:13

For you died, and your life is now hidden with Christ in God.
Colossians 3:3

Acts 4:33, Ephesians 5:2, 1 Corinthians 4:20

43

King's Gallery

Soak in Love

Saturate in My perfect love for *you*, and I will heal your heart. I will set you free with My word, My grace and My truth. My ways are eternal and I came to give you My *life*. Come to Me. Saturate and soak in My intimate love. In the quietness of your heart, I am there. I raise you from dark despair into the light of living hope. Behold My face and take heed to My words, for they are true and faithful. No one has loved you the way I love you. Be still and do not fear. Know My love for you.

"You will know the truth, and the truth will set you free."
John 8:32 HCSB

"Be still and know that I am God. I will be exalted among the nations,
I will be exalted in the earth!"
Psalm 46:10 ESV

Nor height, nor depth, nor any other creature, shall be able to separate us
from the love of God, which is in Christ Jesus our Lord.
Romans 8:39 KJV

King's Gallery

My Gold

My sheep know My voice and they follow Me. Where am I? My heart sees My buried treasure. I sift through pain and brokenness and search for *My gold*. You are My gold and I desire to have you to Myself. 'You are the apple of My eye.' My heart searches for My buried children, My gold. I brush with love, the sand of sin away to reveal that which is covered. Pan with Me and share in the joy of My harvest! The human heart is My most precious creation, and My greatest joy. Oh what treasures you are to Me. I wash the sand of sin and death from you, My precious treasures... And gather you into My heart.

"On the day when I act," says the LORD Almighty, "they will be My treasured possession. I will spare them, just as a father has compassion and spares his son who serves him."
Malachi 3:17

In a desert land he found him, in a barren and howling waste.
He shielded him and cared for him; He guarded him as the apple of his eye.
Deuteronomy 32:10

"Rejoice with me, because I have found my lost sheep! I tell you, in the same way, there will be more joy in heaven over one sinner who repents than over 99 righteous people who don't need repentance."
Luke 15:6-7 HCSB

47

King's Gallery

Faith Bond

Submit to this season, I have your children. I indeed overtake the works of death with My life. Death has no hold on My resurrection power. Do not fear death or the destroyer. My life and power moves through you. Eyes of faith will see My glory manifested in the earth. Even in the darkest depth, I AM there with you. There is a time for everything under the sun. This is a season of 'first things first'. I set in order. I AM a God of order. I set straight that which is broken and right that which is wrong. I use circumstance to forge you. I allow the destroyer to reap havoc to burn away that which occupies the hearts of My beloved. The heat of circumstance brings you to a purity of My life and love for you. Faith is the weld of connection to My perfect love for you. The heat of circumstance creates the bond. I encompass and saturate all things. Nothing is hidden from My eyes. All things are mine and who can take what belongs to Me?

Knowing that the testing of your faith produces endurance.
James 1:3 HCSB

James 1:2-6, Romans 15:13, Ephesians 3:16-17

King's Gallery

Washed in Love

My spirit goes before you. All will melt away like wax, but My words will remain. Heavenly pathways and the highway of holiness is the way to My kingdom. The ways of this world and it's idols will pass away. Cling to My life above all other life pursuits. Become a yielded vessel for My love and glory to be manifested in your world. Release bitterness and anger. Release anything that would compromise the light of My glory and My presence in your life. The power of *presence*... Remember My child and *know* I AM with you. Allow My Spirit to settle and rest on you. Recognize My peace and love. Release all fear. Submit your days and your fears into My hands and I will give you My presence. Lets do this together. I wash your heart and mind, then wrap you up clean in the towel of My love. My children are washed in My love. Clean is what I see and what you are.

So that He might sanctify her, having cleansed her by the washing of water with the word, that He might present to Himself the church in all her glory, having no spot or wrinkle or any such thing; but that she would be holy and blameless.
Ephesians 5:26-27 NASB

Hebrews 10:22, Ezekiel 16:9-10, Luke 21:33, Exodus 33:14

King's Gallery

Miracle Soil

There is a time to work and there is a time to sit and listen. Listening to My words is like soaking in living water. The Son light of My counsel brings forth growth that is heavenward. Growth and fruit do not come from a seed or a caterpillar striving. A miracle takes place in buried submission. Heaven transfers in the nutrients of My presence in those humble hearts that receive My word in peaceful surrender and submission. This is the soil for My miracles.

To every thing there is a season, and a time to every purpose under the heaven.
Ecclesiastes 3:1 KJV

"Submit to God and be at peace with him; in this way prosperity will come to you."
Job 22:21

He performs wonders that cannot be fathomed, miracles that cannot be counted.
Job 5:9

You are the God who performs miracles; you display your power among the peoples.
Psalm 77:14

King's Gallery

Cured

I am calling you to be vessels unto Myself, tried in the furnace of holy fire. Vessels of honor, pots to carry My very presence, *cured* and sealed in the furnace of affliction. Cured of unbelief, cured of fear, cured of pride, cured of self reliance. The oil of My presence will seal the work that I the Lord your God have begun and will accomplish. I will never leave you. The enemy seeks to destroy you with hell fire, but they will be destroyed in My holy fire! Rejoice in the heat of affliction, knowing the moisture of compromise is being burned out. I AM with you in the furnace. Rejoice. My desire is that you be solidified in My love, cured, with no compromise.

Therefore, if anyone cleanses himself from what is dishonorable,
he will be a vessel for honorable use, set apart as holy,
useful to the master of the house, ready for every good work.
2 Timothy 2:21 ESV

Because it is written, Be ye holy; for I am holy.
1 Peter 1:16 KJV

Daniel 3:19-27, Jeremiah 2:13, Romans 12:2

55

King's Gallery

Breaking Forth

I will provide a place for you to break forth like a river. Open to the flow of My spirit and you will open your life to the source of life. I heal that which is broken. I correct that which is crooked. I bring forth beauty from ashes and I resurrect from the dead. *Behold,* My power to save. Stand your ground and do not waiver in unbelief or fear. Lay hold of My life. I give you My perfect love. Watch and see what I will do for you and your family. We are indeed moving towards your season of blessing. Wait for it in hope and peace. This will pass. Set a course for My eternal life...

Then your light will break forth like the dawn,
and your healing will quickly appear; then your righteousness will go before you,
and the glory of the Lord will be your rear guard.
Isaiah 58:8

Yet he saved them for his name's sake, to make his mighty power known.
Psalm 106:8

Therefore I will look unto the LORD;
I will wait for the God of my salvation: my God will hear me.
Micah 7:7 KJV

King's Gallery

Intimate Fruit

Miracle growth breaks forth from My love soil. The anointing is present in that which has been saturated in My presence. Abundant life and power is the natural by-product of intimacy with Me. Miracles are birthed through intimacy. Those who press through to My light and truth, will bring forth the fruit of life. Life *will* spring forth! Continue to soak in My love. Remain in My love and My love will remain in you. Resist the temptation to engage in intimate reflection with fear and lies. What you feed and focus on will grow. So I say to you, focus on My love for you and it will grow. Never give up. Press through the dark soil of your broken life. Press through. Come forth, I say to you, for you have been appointed to be kissed by the 'Son' and be watered from heaven.

But the fruit of the Spirit is love, joy, peace, longsuffering, gentleness, goodness, faith, meekness, temperance: against such there is no law. Galatians 5:22-23 KJV

"Remain in me, as I also remain in you. No branch can bear fruit by itself; it must remain in the vine. Neither can you bear fruit unless you remain in me." John 15:4

King's Gallery

Beauty Seed

The seed of your life may seem insignificant, surrounded in the dirt and darkness of your circumstance. Allow the love of My 'Son-light' to kiss and surround you, even in the brokenness of your life. Abide in My love and My love will abide in you. I tell you the truth, I have designed you to break forth in exquisite beauty. There is a season for everything under the sun. Trust My love above all else and you will indeed see your divine design. My love surrounds and saturates all things. Divine design permeates My creation. Behold My power in the smallest details of life. I AM Faithful and True Love. Plant yourself, your whole self in My love, and I promise you, new life will break forth!

"Very truly I tell you, unless a kernel of wheat falls to the ground and dies, it remains only a single seed. But if it dies, it produces many seeds."
John 12:24

"Shower, O heavens, from above, and let the clouds rain down righteousness; let the earth open, that salvation and righteousness may bear fruit; let the earth cause them both to sprout; I the LORD have created it."
Isaiah 45:8ESV

King's Gallery

Abiding Peace

Why is your heart anxious before Me? Do I not see and understand the smallest details of your life? Why do you fear that I do not see or do not care? My greatest goal was to manifest My love to My beloved. You are My beloved and I desire to bless you with abundant life. Trials of trust are meant to burn away the thieves of My love and the benefits of heaven. Resist the devil and hold fast to My promises, even in the storms of life. There are seasons and times that may seem dark and difficult. Know I stand with you in the furnace and the storms. Nothing will separate you, My beloved, from My eternal love and Life. All opposition and weapons of evil will fail against those who endure and cling to My word. I see your need... Rejoice in the difficulties and great will be your *abiding peace*. Laughter presses through with power in My love and overcomes all things.

The thief comes to only steal and kill and destroy;
I have come that they may have life, and have it to the full.
John 10:10

"Blessed is she who has believed that the Lord would fulfill His promises to her!"
Luke 1:45

He will yet fill your mouth with laughter and your lips with shouts of joy.
Job 8:21

73

King's Gallery

Drink the Pure

Stand fast in this season and be patient. I am moving the pieces into place for your time. Rest and flow in My love and know I see your heart. There is a time for everything under the sun. Your time is coming and I The Lord bring the pieces that make up divine design. Submission to the 'One' leads to the other. I am building your faith and your dependence on that which is reliable. Faithful is your God, despite your fears. I see and deliver you time and time again. See and take note of My Faithful hand. Reject hardness of heart, fear and unbelief. These are robbers of your soul. These are the enemies of heaven and soundness of mind. Reject all lofty thoughts that are contrary to the truth of My love for you. See My pure love in the details of your life. Count your blessings and recognize the many miracles that I The Lord have done and allow me to be *magnified* in your mind. Shut out all that poisons this charge. There are many poisoned water streams... But one that runs pure... Choose *'The One'* to drink from.

"But whoever drinks of the water that I will give him will never be thirsty again.
The water that I will give him will become in him
a spring of water welling up to eternal life."
John 4:14 ESV

John 6:55-56, Psalm 36:8, Matthew 26:27-29

King's Gallery

Heavenly Cell

My instruction will shake awake My bride to her beauty in Me. You will be My blood vessels to carry My life to her. Every prayer pumps My righteous blood to bring life to My beloved. Eyes of faith see what I see. You are supernatural conduits of My kingdom. Count the cost and see the finished harvest of your labor today. Take My yoke in this and your joy will be full. We are all together and nothing will separate you from My love. Watch and see. You will grow in love and I tell you the truth, My presence pumps life to people through your prayers. You are charged with heaven. Apart from Me you can do nothing. Your cell phone with all of its capacity and capability operates by design, but it must sit and receive its charge. Plug in through prayer and communion with My Spirit and you will be *'charged'* with heaven. I have given you a heavenly mandate. Divine instruction from your King to manifest My glory and kingdom… You are My heavenly cell. Sit with Me to be fully charged.

Pray at all times in the Spirit with every prayer and request,
and stay alert in this with all perseverance and intercession for all the saints.
Ephesians 6:18 HCSB

Matthew 6:9-15, 1 Timothy 2:1-6, Matthew 6:7-8

King's Gallery

Sound Alignment

The mind of Christ sees what I see... Child, can your mind lead My body? Complete submission to My will, My word, and My ways brings us together in *sound alignment*. To be *one* in perfect love requires perfect oneness. There is no division in perfect love. Sin causes division to perfect love in your life. Doubt, fear, pride, hate, lust are contrary to My perfect love. Those empty of divisive sin, yielded to My Spirit, will carry the river of My presence. My will is that you would be one, just as I and the Father are one. Complete agreement with the truth creates sound alignment and soundness of mind.

For God hath not given us the spirit of fear; but of power,
and of love, and of a sound mind.
2 Timothy 1:7 KJV

"That all of them may be one, Father, just as you are in me and I am in You.
May they also be in us so that the world may believe that you have sent me.
I have given them the glory that you gave me, that they may be one as we are one—
I in them and you in me—so that they may be brought to complete unity. Then the world
will know that you sent me and have loved them even as you have loved me."
John 17:21-23

King's Gallery

Cellar of Presence

I hide My leaders until the fullness of time, like the finest of wine. Isolation in the cellar of My presence makes the finest wine. Do not fret. There is a day when the wine of your life will open for the world to enjoy in what I have made. I Jesus submitted My life as a carpenter until the right time. Do not be dismayed that you are overlooked. You are hidden in My loving hands and like Joseph, Moses and David. Their time of isolation had a purpose. The taller the leader the deeper the foundation. Trust and submit… When its time, you will know. Work the soil I highlight and rest in My finished work. You were designed to flow from the lap of My victory. All authority in heaven and on earth I give to thee. Tremendous power takes tremendous responsibility. Integrity of character is critical. I build My greatest structures on deep, sound foundations. Yield to Me the areas that compromise your strength and closer we will be to the manifest structure of your destiny.

"Everyone brings out the choice wine first and the cheaper wine after the guests have had too much to drink; but you have saved the best till now."
John 2:10

Philippians 1:6, Luke 10:19, Galatians 4:4-7, Genesis 45:1-3, Proverbs 3:5-6

King's Gallery

Real Fruit

My truth is ever cutting the cancer of compromise and complacency from My sleepy disciples. I shake up and wake up to the reality of the war that wages, and My leaders will indeed understand the hour in which they live. I am calling you to die in the soil of these visions and carry the cross of their reality. Plow with Me and see the fruit to feed the multitude. Movement is required. Steps, real steps of faith pleases Me. Assemble yourselves behind My movement. Paul understood his call as an apostle to the faith, and took up his cross, which brought forth the *real fruit*. All who plow in faith will see a harvest of fruit. Some thirty, some sixty, some one hundredfold. Those who do not plow will not see anything grow.

"You did not choose Me but I chose you, and appointed you that you would go and bear fruit, and that your fruit would remain, so that whatever you ask of the Father in My name He may give to you."
John 15:16-17 NASB

For you were called to this, because Christ also suffered for you, leaving you an example, so that you should follow in His steps.
1 Peter 2:21 HCSB

Matthew 10:38-39, Matthew 13:8, Matthew 26:40, Proverbs 14:23

King's Gallery

Heaven Smiles

Stand in the heat of this trial and do not waiver in My love for you. I have your children and nothing will separate My love from them. Focus on My love for you and do not give heed to fear. My light will expose every wicked lie. My light is dawning in your life. But remember, it is always darkest before the dawn. Stand fast and do not give in to fear and lies. They seek to rob you of My reality that surrounds you. Heaven is here and surrounds you in your circumstance. Even in trouble, I stand with you in the fiery furnace. My resurrection life is in you to face the hounds of hell and death itself. You are My child and you will indeed rise from the ashes. Come closer when things get difficult and I will whisper My love to revive your heart. *Heaven smiles* at My listening saints.

I will declare that your love stands firm forever,
that you have established your faithfulness in heaven itself.
Psalm 89:2

"Do not be afraid of them, for I am with you and will rescue you," declares the LORD.
Jeremiah 1:8

2 Timothy 4:18, Ephesians 6:12

King's Gallery

Heart Hand

Your heart is a hand. What you hold onto effects your very life. Release offense. Release sin. They sicken your soul. Hold My perfect love in the hand of your heart. Release all bitterness and lies that come to occupy the hand of your heart. Release... Lay hold of My perfect love, My truth and My life. Hold My love with all your heart, all your soul, and all your strength. Above all else, is there anything more important than the hand of your heart fully grasping My pure Love for you?

Let all bitterness and wrath and anger and clamor and slander
be put away from you, along with all malice.
Ephesians 4:31 NASB

There is no fear in love; but perfect love casts out fear, because fear involves
punishment, and the one who fears is not perfected in love.
1 John 4:18 NASB

Love the LORD your God with all your heart, with all your soul, and with all your strength.
Deuteronomy 6:5 HCSB

Finally, brethren, whatever is true, whatever is honorable, whatever is right, whatever
is pure, whatever is lovely, whatever is of good repute, if there is any excellence
and if anything worthy of praise, dwell on these things.
Philippians 4:8 NASB

King's Gallery

My Miracles

Saturate in My love for you. Rest the weight of your worries and striving efforts apart, from the abiding that is critical to your peace and well-being. Do not allow other peoples fear and panic effect your heart. You have been called to abide in My love for you. My abiding presence dissipates the darkness of fear and lies. Worship brings the radiance of My glory. Dance and worship Me throughout your day. *My miracles* manifest when they do what they were designed to do. Each after its own kind. You were made in My image. Abide and move in My deep love for you and for others. Nothing you do is more beautiful in My eyes. Plant yourself in the source of love and life and you will look like True Love.

Cast all your anxiety on him, because he cares for you.
1 Peter 5:7

Yet a time is coming and has now come when the true worshipers will worship the Father in the Spirit and in truth, for they are the kind of worshipers the Father seeks.
John 4:23

So God created man in His own image; in the image of God He created him; male and female He created them.
Genesis 1:27 NASB

89

King's Gallery

Narrow Way

Rejoice in the details of this day and prepare thyself for what I am about to do. We are turning the corner for many of My children and things will look quite different. Remove the clutter and weight of the world and above all learn to hear My love for you. Narrow is the way that leads to life and few find it. Simplify your life and your focus. Obedience to My Spirit is the only path to life and eternal treasures. Come away often to settle in My Presence and allow Me to calibrate your heart, your mind and your schedule. All activity outside of My presence and purpose is chasing the wind. The evidence of My life power is clearly established and confirmed by many signs and wonders. Ignorance is no excuse for a life that never seeks its maker. *Truth* can be examined from every angle and will stand the test of time and scrutiny.

This is the day that the LORD has made; let us rejoice and be glad in it.
Psalm 118:24 ESV

"Enter through the narrow gate; for the gate is wide and the way is broad that leads to destruction, and there are many who enter through it. For the gate is small and the way is narrow that leads to life, and there are few who find it."
Matthew 7:13-14 NASB

Romans 6:16 , Deuteronomy 28:1 , 1 Kings 11:38

Due Season

You are in a time of refreshing and change. My presence and power will manifest the atmosphere of heaven in and around the world you walk. Simply look to Me your shepherd and My love will carry you through its field. Flowers and fruit come forth by My divine design planted deep in the soil. Vision seeds break forth in the earth of your hearts and minds planted by My love for you. My reign and My Son bring forth its productive beauty as you reach heavenward in prayer. Humble hearts make the best soil for great growth. By My timing and seasons, miracle growth happens. Maturity is a process of submission. Trust My ability to bring forth what's needed in *due season*.

Thy kingdom come. Thy will be done in earth, as it is in heaven.
Matthew 6:10 KJV

"Even to your old age and gray hairs I am he, I am he who will sustain you.
I have made you and I will carry you; I will sustain you and I will rescue you."
Isaiah 46:4

Humble yourselves therefore under the mighty hand of God,
that he may exalt you in due time.
1 Peter 5:6 KJV

Song of Solomon 2:12, Ezekiel 34:25-31

93

King's Gallery

Open Confidence

There are times of testing your faith. You are in such a time. Where is your confidence? How big is your God? How many dire situations have I the Lord delivered My children from? Put your loss and your lack in My hands. My provision and My protection are supernatural. You must see beyond the natural ways of provision. I AM your provider, and nothing can stop My provision. Open wide your confidence by faith. Like wings, faith is wide *open confidence* in a big God. Your ability to see how big I AM comes from you soaking in My word and My testimonies. Faith comes by hearing, and hearing the word of God. Faith, or wide open confidence comes from seeing My power and My faithfulness, even in dire circumstances, even death. Who is like the Lord your God? That is the point. If there is a war, and there is, where is your confidence? Life or death? Who's words do you believe? What moves you, fear or Love? This is the foundation for life or death.

"But blessed is the one who trusts in the LORD, whose confidence is in him."
Jeremiah 17:7

Matthew 17:20, Matthew 19:26, Romans 10:17, James 1:3

King's Gallery

Life Carpenter

Do not be dismayed by the desolation that is to come. For that which is temporary must be taken out of the way to make room for that which is eternal. The temporary will exchange for the eternal. Extreme home makeover of the heart must happen with the demolition of the old and decaying. Pride is like termites to the structural integrity of the human heart. I AM doing a new thing. Those who follow close by My spirit will witness miracles and see the resurrection of a nation. Those who call on My name will see their King of glory come in. I created the destroyer which reaps havoc. I even use for good those blinded by evil to bring about My divine purpose. Invasive is the surgery that cuts out the cancer that preserves the life of My children. Eyes of faith will see My hand move and the miracles that follow. Do not be dismayed at the desolation, but know I hold the plans for new life. 'The kingdom of God is at hand' My children. I alone bring beauty from your ashes and even death can not stop My love.

"So do not fear, for I am with you; do not be dismayed, for I am your God.
I will strengthen you and help you; I will uphold you with my righteous right hand."
Isaiah 41:10

Matthew 7:24-27, Jeremiah 29:11, Ezekiel 18:31-32, Psalm 51:10

King's Gallery

Your Shepherd

This is a season of learning to wait upon My voice. When the storms of thought and the waves of circumstance clamor for your attention, rest and wait to hear My still small voice. Allow My Spirit to heighten your supernatural senses. Rest in My peace and you *will* hear My voice. Your openness will increase your ability. Bring yourself back to Me, *Your shepherd*. I watch over your very life. My sheep know My voice. It is My purpose and plan to lead you to good things. Stay close to Me. I lead you to green pastures—abundant life and beside the still waters—perfect peace. The purpose and foundation of your very life was created to be in unbroken communion with Me, your shepherd.

The LORD is my shepherd; I shall not want. He makes me lie down in green pastures. He leads me beside still waters. He restores my soul. He leads me in paths of righteousness for his name's sake. Even though I walk through the valley of the shadow of death, I will fear no evil, for you are with me; your rod and your staff, they comfort me.
Psalm 23:1-4 ESV

"My sheep hear My voice, and I know them, and they follow Me."
John 10:27 NASB

John 10:11, Hebrews 13:20-21, John 21:16-17

King's Gallery

Turning to Love

A tool with integrity gets used much. Reliable is My design. Soundness of mind is a mind that does not leak through broken ways. Integrity is a vessel that is sealed and carries the fullness of My ways. Cooperation with My Spirit brings soundness of mind. Do not worry about tomorrow, but be obedient to what I give you today. Release your worries to Me. Cracked pots lack integrity and the ability to carry the ways of My kingdom. To come into alignment with My kingdom is to bring the broken pieces of your life, your broken ways into divine order. Integrity and soundness of mind are vessels of My perfect love. Repentance is turning to My ways...

Therefore, if anyone cleanses himself from what is dishonorable,
he will be a vessel for honorable use, set apart as holy,
useful to the master of the house, ready for every good work.
2 Timothy 2:21 ESV

For to be carnally minded is death; but to be spiritually minded is life and peace.
Romans 8:6 KJV

Psalm 25:21, Proverbs 10:9, Jeremiah 2:13

King's Gallery

Eternal Seed

Everywhere you go and everywhere you are is My harvest. My body, the seed of My kingdom is planted in the soil of My children, those born of My Spirit. You carry My sincere love to the places I your God have planted you. Release the seed I have given you into the dying soil of those around you, that My *life* would multiply and manifest. Eternal is My harvest that bares the fruit of My true love.

He told them: "The harvest is abundant, but the workers are few.
Therefore, pray to the Lord of the harvest to send out workers into His harvest."
Luke 10:2 HCSB

For you have been born again not of seed which is perishable but imperishable,
that is, through the living and enduring word of God.
1 Peter 1:23 NASB

Now He who supplies seed to the sower and bread for food will supply and multiply
your seed for sowing and increase the harvest of your righteousness.
2 Corinthians 9:10 NASB

King's Gallery

Path of Light

Those who deceive are on slippery ground. Do I not see? All who cling to evil and deceit will be disciplined by their own ways. Darkness will indeed surround them. Unless they turn to My mercy and love, they will perish in darkness. Today is the day of salvation. Today if you hear My voice, what My Spirit is saying, do not harden your heart. I AM the creator of *all things*. All who reject Me, love death. Judgment is here and truth and light will vanquish lies and darkness. Sin and lies are exposed in the light of truth. I have lit your path with My presence. I AM the way, the truth, and the life.

Jesus answered, "The light will be with you only a little longer.
Walk while you have the light so that darkness doesn't overtake you.
The one who walks in darkness doesn't know where he's going."
John 12:35 HCSB

Jesus said to him, "I am the way, and the truth, and the life;
no one comes to the Father but through Me."
John 14:6 NASB

John 3:19, Psalm 94:9, Romans 12:9

King's Gallery

Layers of Glory

Beauty, joy and freedom will attract the lost and lonely. Layers of My glory will wash the landscape of darkness and expose its hidden beauty. Now is the time of My rising and no eye has seen what I the Lord have prepared for those who love Me. You will see My faithful hand in your life and I will bless you with True Love, 'on earth as it is in heaven'. You will share what I The Lord have put within you, for it is for My glory that I share with you, that many would taste and see My goodness. None compare to My True Love.

The heavens declare the glory of God; the skies proclaim the work of his hands.
Psalm 19:1

We all, with unveiled faces, are looking as in a mirror at the glory of the Lord
and are being transformed into the same image from glory to glory;
this is from the Lord who is the Spirit.
2 Corinthians 3:18 HCSB

Restore us, LORD God Almighty; make your face shine on us, that we may be saved.
Psalm 80:19

Your kingdom come, your will be done, on earth as it is in heaven.
Matthew 6:10

King's Gallery

Place of Fullness

Sink into the River bottom of My Spirit, and let Me fill you with the deep things of heaven. I am not lofty by the worlds standards. I indeed encompass all things and dwell in the heights of eternity, but also in the hearts of the humble. Like pyramids in the dry desert, a picture of the pride of man. Tiny dry triangles, full of dead mans bones. Isolated islands of rebellion, separate from My eternal life. Flatten and empty yourself of all pride. Dig deep, the sand of your mind down low, to find My heart and I will fill you.

"Whoever believes in me,
as scripture has said, rivers of living water will flow from within them."
John 7:38

For thus says the One who is high and lifted up, who inhabits eternity, whose name
is Holy: "I dwell in the high and holy place, and also with him who is of a contrite and
lowly spirit, to revive the spirit of the lowly, and to revive the heart of the contrite."
Isaiah 57:15 ESV

Philippians 2:6-7, Matthew 23:27, John 15:4, Isaiah 44:3, Matthew 11:29

King's Gallery

Vision Wings

You are indeed coming into the manifestation of *vision wings*. Cocoon in this final season. I have created this time for you to bring forth its details. Redeem the time in My grace. Ride on the roots of My love and you will rise. Shut out fear and lies and do not take heed to the voice of death. Light does not run from darkness, but darkness runs from light. Meditate and soak in My promises and keep the joy set before you of My manifest glory. You are My instrument of creation. I bring the parts together that make up the miracle of life. Laugh at lies and they will flee. Laugh I say, My *life* defies death.

I am sure of this, that He who started a good work in you will carry it on
to completion until the day of Christ Jesus.
Philippians 1:6 HCSB

"And you will know the truth, and the truth will set you free."
John 8:32 ESV

Romans 8:20-23, Gen. 1:27, Ephesians 2:10

KING'S
GALLERY

'A Place of Real Hope'

King's Gallery

Evidence

www.kingsgallerylivingwords.com/evidence is an online display of the glory of God.

The proof of God is found in the profound depth of *evidence*—powerful testimonies from around the world of the *real* God of the universe, healing and touching lives and bringing beauty from ashes. Jesus is the same 'yesterday, today and forever'. There is simply no other name in human history that is so completely surrounded by signs, wonders and miracles than the name of Jesus Christ. The sheer number of miracles underscores the testimonies of the original disciples and the testimony of Jesus Himself that He is truly the Son of the living God and the True Savior of the world. Let the evidence speak for itself to all 'with ears to hear and eyes to see.'

Visit **www.kingsgallerylivingwords.com/evidence** to see the growing collection of video testimonies and documentaries that demonstrate the truth and the power of True Love—'God with us'.

King's Gallery

Open Confidence

There are times of testing your faith. You are in such a time. Where is your confidence? How big is your God? How many dire situations have I the Lord delivered My children from? Put your loss and your lack in My hands. My provision and My protection are Supernatural. You must see beyond the natural ways of provision. I AM your provider, and nothing can stop My provision. Open wide your confidence by faith. Like wings, faith is wide *open confidence* in a big God. Your ability to see how big I AM comes from you soaking in My Word and My testimonies. Faith comes by hearing, and hearing the Word of God. Faith, or wide open confidence comes from seeing My power and My faithfulness, even in dire circumstances, even death. Who is like the Lord your God? That is the point… If there is a war, and there is, where is your confidence? Life or death? Who's words do you believe? What moves you, fear or Love? This is the foundation for life or death.

"But blessed is the one who trusts in the LORD, whose confidence is in him."

King's Galler

Cocoon

How big is your God child? *Cocoon* in the light of My Presence. Allow saturate your mind with heavens reality. I will show you a better way. Com submission to the cocoon of divine design is the only pathway to its r Relinquish all of your crawling ways. Attach to Me, The Vine, and cocoon Love. I will transform your heart. Allow Me to download your divine pu Quietly submit and attach to My Love. Listen to the inspiration of My Spir Voice…

"Behold, I AM the LORD, the God of all flesh. Is anything too hard for Me?"
Jeremiah 32:27 ESV

Do not conform to the pattern of this world, but be transformed by the renewing of your mind. Then you will be able to test and approve what God's will is—his good, pleasing and perfect will.
Romans 12:2

He will transform the body of our humble condition into the likeness of His glorious body, by the power that enables Him to subject everything to Himself
Philippians 3:21 HCSB

Ark of Presence

Soak in My instruction each day, then move out. Let the water of My Words carry your boat into your day, it beats rowing on the sand of self. The Ark of My Presence is the structure that carries the life. All activity outside the 'Ark' of My presence leads to death. Abide in My Love and My Wisdom. Divine design and destiny are accomplished when you are in alignment with My Will and My Word.

But seek ye first the kingdom of God, and his righteousness;
and all these things shall be added unto you.
Matthew 6:33 KJV

As the Father has loved me, so have I loved you. Abide in my love.
John 15:9 ESV

Listen to my instruction and be wise; do not disregard it.
Proverbs 8:33

By faith Noah, when warned about things not yet seen,
in holy fear built an ark to save his family.
Hebrews 11:7

the splendor of our God.
Isaiah 35:2

(John 7:38, 2 Chronicles 7:14)

Order Canvas Prints

Order canvas prints of your favorite *Living* Words as seen in this book.

Hang them on your living room wall, near your bed or in your entry way to serve as a daily visual reminder of Gods promises, comfort and uplifting encouragement.

Available in one size 32" X 16" with a 1.25" depth.

Place your orders at **www.kingsgallerylivingwords.com**.